S E N E G A L

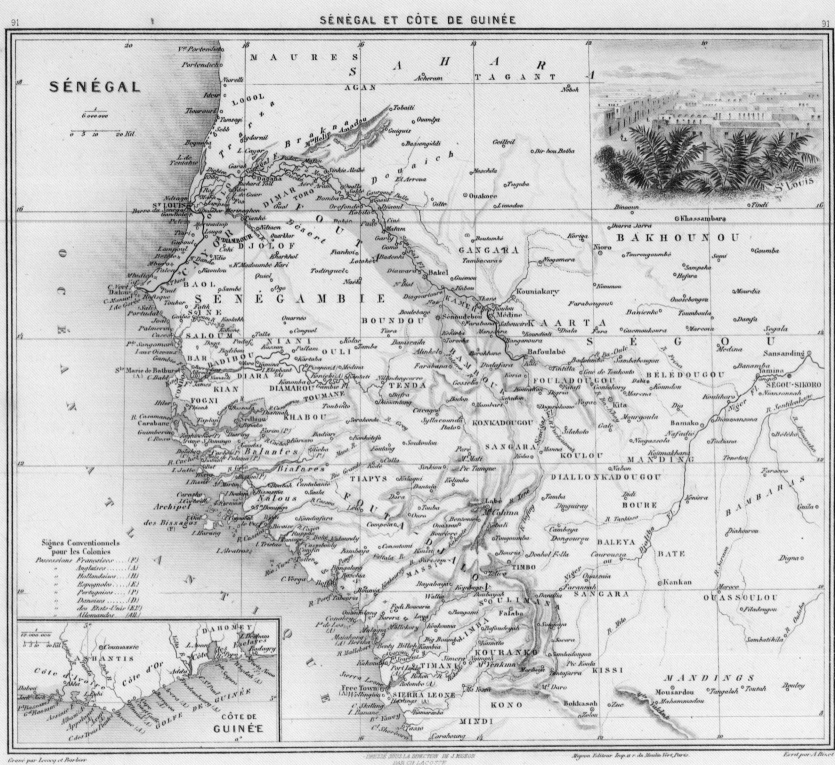

MAP OF SENEGAL CIRCA 1889

SENEGAL

A COUNTRY AND ITS PEOPLE

PHOTOGRAPHS BY AKIHIRO YAMAMURA
INTRODUCTION BY MOHAMED MBODJ

TAKARAJIMA BOOKS

Takarajima Books

200 Varick Street

New York, NY 10014

Tel:

[212] 675-1944

Fax:

[212] 255-5731

Book and jacket design by Archie Ferguson

Editor: Susan Bell

Takarajima Books Publisher: Akihiko Miyanaga

Assistant Publisher: Kiyotaka Yaguchi

ISBN: 1-883489-12-1

Library of Congress Card Number: 94-060222

Printed and bound by

Toppan Printing Co.,[Shenzhen] Ltd., China

ACKNOWLEDGMENTS

I would like to thank the following people who helped make this project possible: most especially, Mà Amparo Aranda, for her generous support in coordinating my first travels to Senegal; Pizzo Gianpietro and Andreina Visconti for their knowledgeable assistance in Senegal; Rumiko Abe and Salvatore Cabras, my travel companions. Thanks also to Fumiaki Tanaka at Nikon; Dr. Mohamed Mbodj for contributing the text; Kenichiro Tominaga at Takarajimasha, Tokyo and Akihiko Miyanaga at Takarajima Books, New York; Susan Bell for her editing; and Archie Ferguson for his design.

Finally, to all the Senegalese people who stood in front of my camera, thank you—merci beaucoup!

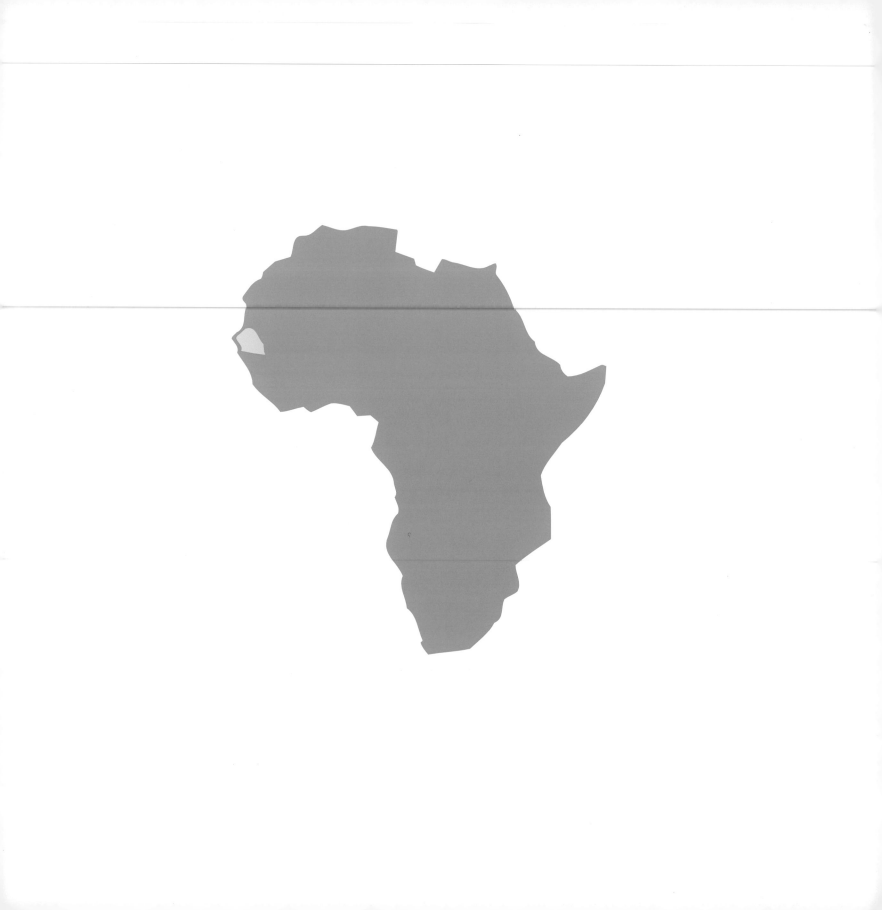

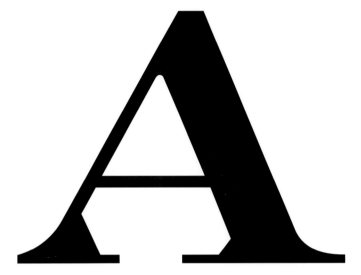A SMALL, VIBRANT COUNTRY, SENEGAL SITS AT THE WESTERNMOST POINT OF AFRICA, THRIVING IN THE PRESENT, AND AT THE SAME TIME MAINTAINING ITS HISTORICALLY RICH TRADITIONS. IT HAS BEEN INHABITED CONTINUOUSLY FOR THE LAST ONE HUNDRED FIFTY THOUSAND YEARS. SENEGAL'S FIRST STATE, GHANA, APPEARED ON THE NORTHERN BANK OF THE SENEGAL RIVER, EXPANDING SLOWLY TOWARDS THE SOUTH AND WEST. IN 1445, THE PORTUGUESE ARRIVED, AND BY 1510 OR SO OCCUPIED AN ISLAND OFF THE COAST CALLED GORÉE. IT IS SAID THAT THE NAME "SENEGAL" COMES FROM THE WOLOF TERM FOR DUGOUT CANOE, AS IT WAS MISPRONOUNCED BY THE VISITING PORTUGUESE SAILORS IN THE MIDDLE OF THE FIFTEENTH CENTURY.

DUTCH, FRENCH AND BRITISH EXPLORERS SOON FOLLOWED, AND THE COMPETITION AMONG THE LATTER TWO FOR IMPERIAL CONTROL BECAME FIERCE. IN 1659, THE FRENCH, GAINING AN EDGE OVER THE BRITISH AND THE DUTCH, SETTLED THE ISLAND OF SAINT-LOUIS AT THE MOUTH OF THE SENEGAL RIVER. BY THE LATE 1800S THEY HAD COLONIZED THE WHOLE COUNTRY, THE BRITISH KEEPING THE LOWER VALLEY OF THE GAMBIA RIVER, WHICH BECAME TODAY'S REPUBLIC OF GAMBIA.

AS THE AFRICAN COUNTRY CLOSEST TO THE UNITED STATES, SENEGAL AND ITS GORÉE ISLAND USED TO BE THE LAST SPOT OF MOTHERLAND THE UNFORTUNATE SLAVE BOUND TO THE AMERICAS COULD SEE.

Senegal became the centerpiece of French colonial rule in Africa; and both culturally and architecturally, the French left their mark. Some of the most well-preserved colonial buildings on the entire continent remain in Senegal's coastal towns. Saint-Louis was the headquarters of French possessions in Black Africa, succeeded by Dakar in 1902. Saint-Louis had the largest European community in West Africa, and a sizable number of Senegalese enjoyed full French citizenship.

Since Senegal attained independence on April 4, 1960, it has enjoyed remarkable stability and a democratic regime, despite some political upheavals and a struggling economy. It has also maintained strong, friendly ties with France.

In Senegal, contradictions between old and new, between indigenous and European, flourish in an unusual atmosphere of tolerance, respect and harmony. A diverse group of religions and ethnic communities live together there peacefully.

By the end of the eighth century, Islam arrived, and, traveling from the North to the South, eventually became the country's dominant religion. Serer and Joola tribes aside, ninety percent of Senegalese are Muslim. East facing mosques, with their radiant domes, thus pervade the country's landscape (p. 43). Islam profited from the traditional local African religions, which, like itself, identified a unique, paramount God associated with other lesser deities, and believed in the immortality of the soul. Most Senegambians did not place an emphasis on cult objects, preferring, like Muslims, more spiritual forms of adoration. They also shared with Islam a belief in polygamy, circumcision, and a community oriented economy.

About five percent of the Senegalese are Roman Catholic, many of whom live in the southwestern corner of the country, in lower Casamance. The cohabitation of these radically different religious groups is notable, as their accord is not superficial or distant: it is not unusual to find both religions in the same village, or even the same family. Indeed, Senegal was perhaps, for some twenty years, the only overwhelmingly Muslim country to have a practicing Catholic as its President. And while the current president is Muslim, his wife is a practicing Catholic.

Schooling, too, blends the two religions. I was born and raised in Dakar, Senegal's capital and biggest city; like most of my friends, I had two years at the local Koranic school,

LEARNING TO READ AND MEMORIZE THE KORAN; AND THEN, AT SIX, I WENT TO THE FRENCH CATHOLIC ELE-MENTARY SCHOOL. MANY URBAN PARENTS TODAY SEND THEIR CHILDREN DIRECTLY TO FRENCH SCHOOL.

DESPITE THE MODERN INFLUENCES OF ISLAM AND CHRISTIANITY, SENEGALESE STILL PRACTICE DEVOTION TO THE SPIRITS THAT WERE AN ESSENTIAL PART OF TRADITIONAL LOCAL RELIGIONS. IN THE OLD DAYS, LIBATIONS AND SACRIFICES WERE PERFORMED TO RELIEVE ANXIETY OR CURE ILLNESS. LIBATIONS REMAIN AN ESSENTIAL PART OF LIFE IN SENEGAL. PERFORMED BY LOCAL SHAMANS, THEY PURIFY AND PROTECT AGAINST MEAN SPIRITS OR BAD LUCK. IN A WRESTLING MATCH, FOR EXAMPLE, THE WRESTLER, IT IS BELIEVED, FIGHTS NOT JUST HIS HUMAN OPPONENT, BUT PERNICIOUS SPIRITS; AND SO HE UNDERGOES A LIBATION RITUAL BEFORE THE MATCH TO WARD THEM OFF (PP. 54, 55).

AS A CHILD GROWING UP IN SENEGAL, MY LIFE, LIKE THE LIVES AROUND ME, REVOLVED AROUND MEALS, GAMES AND CHORES. DINNERS CONSISTED OF STEWED MEAT IN A SAUCE OVER SORGHUM, OR FRIED FISH. MIDDAY MEALS MEANT RICE WITH FISH, SORGHUM PORRIDGE, OR GRITS WITH MILK. WE HAD A SIMPLE BREAKFAST OF HERBAL TEA, MILK, AND BUTTERED FRENCH BREAD. RURAL VILLAGERS TEND TO EAT MORE LOCALLY GROWN CEREALS, WHILE CITY DWELLERS ARE ACCUSTOMED TO RICE IMPORTED FROM INDOCHINA. TODAY'S MOST COMMON DISHES, CONSIDERED NATIONAL SPECIALTIES, ARE RICE WITH FISH AND VEGETABLES STEWED IN TOMATO SAUCE; CHICKEN MARINATED IN LEMON JUICE OVER RICE; AND RICE SMOTHERED IN PEANUT BUTTER SAUCE. KOLA NUTS ARE A REVERED PART OF THE SENEGALESE DIET. AFTER MEALS, GUESTS SHARE THEM, AS A DIGESTIVE AND STIMULANT. IMPORTED FROM AS FAR AS THE IVORY COAST AND LIBERIA, KOLA NUTS ARE CONSIDERED SACRED, AND ARE THUS SHARED TO CELEBRATE WEDDINGS AND BAPTISMS, PERFORM DIVINATIONS, AND SEAL BUSINESS DEALS.

WHEN I WAS A BOY, THE TEA SESSION AFTER MOST MEALS WAS MY FAVORITE TIME OF DAY. THE WHOLE FAMILY AND GUESTS WOULD GATHER AROUND A SMALL CHARCOAL BURNER AND TEA POT FOR AN HOUR OR MORE, SLOWLY DRINKING A HOT SWEET DECOCTION OF CHINESE GREEN TEA AND PEPPERMINT LEAVES, AND EATING SALTED ROASTED PEANUTS, FRESH BREAD OR DRIED MEAT. THESE WERE PRECIOUS MOMENTS TO DISCUSS AND DECIDE THINGS, LAUGH, AND FEEL COMMUNAL WARMTH.

THE EXTENDED FAMILY OF MY CHILDHOOD IS DISAPPEARING FROM SENEGAL'S BIG TOWNS, BUT REMAINS PREVALENT IN THE COUNTRYSIDE, WHERE ONE FAMILY COULD INCLUDE A WHOLE VILLAGE. I GREW UP, WITH MY BROTHERS AND SISTERS, IN A HOUSE CROWDED WITH UNCLES, AUNTS, GREAT AUNTS,

GRANDPARENTS AND COUSINS. CHILDREN WERE AT THE CENTER OF FAMILY LIFE, WITH EVERYBODY SHARING IN THEIR REARING. MY GRANDMA AND GREAT AUNT USED TO TELL ME BEDTIME STORIES, WHILE MY UNCLES SUPERVISED MY HOMEWORK.

THE INITIATION RITE OF YOUNG MALES FROM TEENAGERS TO ADULTHOOD IS DISAPPEARING FROM THE CITIES, BUT REMAINS AN IMPORTANT PART OF RURAL LIFE—ESPECIALLY IN THE SOUTHERN JOOLA AND BASSARI SOCIETIES. IN THE CITIES, CIRCUMCISION IS NOW PERFORMED ON BABIES OR JUST BEFORE A BOY STARTS SCHOOL, WHEREAS IN THE COUNTRYSIDE YOUNG MEN ARE CIRCUMCISED IN THEIR INITIATION INTO MANHOOD. THE DAY BEFORE THE OPERATION, USUALLY PERFORMED BY THE LOCAL BLACKSMITH—THOUGH INCREASINGLY A NURSE OR DOCTOR IS INVOLVED—THE INITIATES RECEIVE THEIR CHOICE OF MEAL, SHAVE THEIR HEADS AND ARE FETED BY CLOSE FAMILY. TO PROVE THEY ARE MATURE, THE BOYS MUST SHOW NO SIGN OF SUFFERING WHEN THE CIRCUMCISION IS PERFORMED. AFTERWARD, AMID A DANCING CROWD, THE BOYS RETREAT INTO THE NEARBY BUSH OR FOREST. THERE THEY REMAIN, UNDER CLOSE SUPERVISION OF OLDER GUARDIANS, FOR THREE TO FOUR WEEKS. THE GUARDIANS TEACH THEM TO FIGHT, HUNT, BE PATIENT, SPEAK WELL, BEHAVE PROPERLY WITH WOMEN AND ELDERS, AND, IN GENERAL, BE A GOOD MEMBER OF THE COMMUNITY. THEY INCULCATE THEM WITH LOCAL HISTORY, SURVIVAL TIPS, AND A STRONG SENSE OF PRIDE, BOTH AS INDIVIDUALS AND MEMBERS OF SOCIETY. AT THE END OF THE SECLUSION, THE BOYS—NOW DEEMED MEN—COME OUT DRESSED IN THEIR FINEST AND DANCING. IN AN ITINERANT DANCE PARTY, THEY VISIT EACH OTHER'S FAMILIES, RECEIVING GIFTS AND NEW CLOTHES. AFTER A FEAST OF A FEW DAYS, THE YOUNG MEN MUST FACE THE FIRST STEPS OF ADULTHOOD: STARTING A FAMILY OF THEIR OWN, AND PARTICIPATING IN MEETINGS OF THE VILLAGE ELDERS.

DANCE PLAYS AN ESSENTIAL ROLE IN SENEGAL, AS A PART OF MANY RITES AND FESTIVALS OF WHICH INITIATION IS JUST ONE. WRESTLING VICTORIES, HARVESTS, BAPTISMS, FOR EXAMPLE, ALL INVOLVE DANCING. IN MOST VILLAGES OR SUBURBS, AN ORGANIZING COMMITTEE EXISTS TO CHOOSE THE DATE, THE MUSICIANS AND THE SITE FOR DANCE PARTIES. DANCE IS NOT PERMITTED IN FARMING SEASON, NOR ON OTHER SPECIAL DAYS. THE BAND CONSISTS OF AT LEAST THREE, AND USUALLY FIVE TO SEVEN, PROFESSIONAL DRUMMERS. SOMETIMES ANOTHER INSTRUMENT, AFRICAN OR EUROPEAN, JOINS THEM. THE VENUE IS A SANDY AREA IN THE MIDDLE OF THE VILLAGE OR AT A CROSSROADS IN TOWN. A HUMAN CIRCLE IS FORMED. THE YOUNGEST SIT ON THE SAND IN THE INNER CIRCLE. BEHIND THEM, WOMEN SIT OR STAND. MEN, STANDING, FORM AN OUTER CIRCLE. BOYS, GIRLS AND WOMEN CLAP WITH WOOD OR METAL CLAPPERS. THE MUSICIANS, DRESSED IN THEIR BEST CLOTHES, FACE THE GUESTS WHO WILL GIVE THEM AND THE BEST DANCERS MONEY.

NORMALLY, ONLY GIRLS, WOMEN, AND BOYS DANCE, BUT IN THE WOLOF COUNTRY, MEN DANCE AS WELL. OFTEN DANCERS COMMUNE WITH NATURE, IMITATING ANIMALS, SUCH AS PELICANS IN FLIGHT (P. 35). DANCE, WHICH TAKES PLACE AT RITES EITHER JOYOUS OR PAINFUL, PROVIDES A POWERFUL SENSE OF COMMUNITY UNITY.

THE SENEGALESE LIKE TO DRESS UP DURING CELEBRATIONS. INDEED, THEY HAVE THE DISTINCTION OF PRODUCING SOME OF THE FINEST CLOTH AND CLOTHES, AS WELL AS JEWELRY, IN BLACK AFRICA. THE PRIMARY FABRIC USED IS LOCAL COTTON, EITHER PRINTED OR TIE-DYED. PRINTED FABRIC IS WORN EVERY-DAY, WHILE THE DYED OR HAND WOVEN KIND IS RESERVED FOR SPECIAL OCCASIONS. DYING IS A HIGHLY VALUED SKILL PASSED FROM MOTHER TO DAUGHTER (PP. 96, 97). WEAVING SKILLS GET PASSED AMONG THE FAMILY MEN. SENEGALESE DRESS VARIES ACCORDING TO OCCASION. AFTER WORK, MEN WEAR THE "BUBU," A LONG MUSLIM GOWN, OVER A SHIRT AND SHORTS. THE OUTFIT IS COMPLETED BY LEATHER LOAFERS AND A HAT—A RED FEZ, A GRASS HAT, OR A WOVEN COTTON ONE. WOMEN WEAR A RADIANTLY COLORED BUBU, TIED AROUND THE WAIST WITH A SARONG-LIKE WRAPPER—THE MORE COMPLICATED THE TIE THE BETTER. A HEAD SCARF MATCHES THE COLOR AND DESIGN OF THEIR BUBU. TRADITIONAL COSTUME IS OCCASIONALLY WORN, ALWAYS WITH A SENSE OF CEREMONY, SUCH AS THE REAMS OF LUSCIOUS COLOR DONNED BY WOMEN WATCHING THE LEGENDARY PIROGUE RACES (P. 53). THE DELICACY OF TEXTILE PATTERNS AND SOPHISTICA-TION OF DESIGN IN SENEGAL PUT THE COUNTRY AT THE FOREFRONT OF FASHION IN BLACK AFRICA.

AN IMPORTANT ASPECT OF GROOMING AND FASHION IS HAIR (P. 59). GIRLS AS YOUNG AS A FEW MONTHS OLD HAVE THEIR HAIR BRAIDED WITH BEADS AND OTHER SMALL OBJECTS. BOYS HAVE THEIR HAIR CUT IN A STYLE THAT MAY REFLECT THE FAMILY THEY COME FROM, THIER AGE OR THEIR ETHNIC IDENTITY. INDEED, ALONG WITH THE ART OF THE JEWELER (WHO WORKS WITH GOLD, SILVER, IRON AND COPPER) AND THE TAILOR, THE PANACHE OF THE HAIRDRESSER IS AMONG SENEGAL'S MOST VALUED TALENTS, EXPORTED TO AFRICA, EUROPE AND AMERICA.

EVERY SENEGALESE VILLAGE OR TOWN HAS AT ITS CENTER A MOSQUE AND, NEXT TO IT, AN OPEN AIR MARKET (PP. 24, 25). THE MARKET IS MORE THAN A PLACE OF COMMERCE. IT IS A SOCIAL CENTER, WHERE ONE GATHERS TO TALK AND PLAY GAMES. IT IS COMMON TO FIND PEOPLE THERE PLAYING AFRICAN CHESS OR EUROPEAN CHECKERS UNDER THE SHADE OF A BIG TREE. TRADITIONAL CHECKERS REQUIRES EACH PLAYER TO OFFER A PROVERB OR APHORISM ALONG WITH EACH MOVE; THE CIRCLE OF ONLOOKERS JUDGES HIS REMARK RELEVANT OR NOT. A WINNER EMERGES WHEN HIS OPPONENT HAS EITHER LOST THE LAST OF HIS PAWNS, OR RUN OUT OF WIT.

Most houses in rural or suburban Senegal are constructed from mud, straw, thatch and wood. These materials are combined to produce various kinds of adobe style dwellings (pp. 30, 42, 50), in an architectural style called "Sudanese." In the cities, professional builders use bricks and industrial cement. In general, men build houses, women decorate and maintain them.

Just over seventy six thousand square miles and with some eight million inhabitants, the country sustains itself mainly through agriculture and fishing. Indeed, the infamous Senegalese markets are some of the most varied, colorful and abundant in the world. In the north, sorghum, millet, peas and peanuts are main crops; in the south, farmers grow rice, maize, peanuts, sorghum and cotton. Home grown produce goes to the local markets, while peanuts and cotton are commercial crops destined for industrialized transformation and export abroad.

Farming takes place on small family plots, with every adult member owning a piece of the farm, and everyone in the family pitching in to tend the plot. At peak planting and harvest times, villagers help each other out, using their simple tools of hoe and horse drawn till. Chemical fertilizers and tractors are hard to find in Senegal. Manure, too, is shunned as fertilizer; farmers prefer to burn wild grasses before the rainy season, using the ashes to fertilize a soil that is often sandy and fragile. About twenty miles from Dakar is the "garden belt," where huge quantities of flowers and vegetables are grown for domestic consumption and export. Men farm and handle export sales; women control domestic sales. Vegetable gardens near family homes are tended by women, who plant tomatoes, okra, herbs, parsley and more, for their family's daily needs.

Besides vegetables and grains, fruit is one of Senegal's riches. A wide market offers not just the predictable pineapple, banana, and mango, but also palm kernels from Casamance, and the baobab fruit from the country's center and north. The baobab tree (adansonia digitata) is remarkable at forty to sixty feet tall and thirty feet across the width of its trunk (p. 37). The largest trees have sacred status. Baobab trees stand alone in the middle of a village or in clusters on a plain, helping to define the Senegalese landscape and way of life. The Wolof and the Serer tribes use the edible pulp for medicine, soap, rope, and fertilizer, while the hollowed trunks are used for canoes or as shelter for the traveler or runaway.

MOREOVER, ACCORDING TO THE COUNTRY'S LORE, THE BAOBAB, ALONG WITH THE TAMARIND, IS A FAVORITE SPOT FOR GENIES AND SPIRITS.

AFTER FARMING, FISHING IS THE LARGEST OF SENEGAL'S INDIGENOUS INDUSTRIES, AND IS CURRENTLY THE LEADING SOURCE OF EXPORT REVENUE. SENEGALESE ARE AMONG THE BIGGEST FISH EATERS IN THE WORLD, SECOND ONLY TO THE JAPANESE. WOMEN RUN THE DOMESTIC FISH MARKETS, WHILE MEN, EQUIPPED WITH MOTORIZED DUGOUT CANOES AND TRAILING NETS, CATCH THE FISH AND EXPORT THEM TO EUROPE AND OTHER AFRICAN COUNTRIES (PP. 82, 83). WOMEN SUPERVISE THE SMOKING, SALTING AND DRYING THAT MUCH OF THE FISH UNDERGOES. PRESERVED FISH ARE SOLD AS FAR AS ONE HUNDRED MILES AWAY FROM WHERE THEY WERE CAUGHT. WITH THEIR TWO HUNDRED FIFTY MILE COASTLINE, AND MANY LAKES AND RIVERS, THE SENEGALESE HAVE, NOT SURPRISINGLY, DEVELOPED A CONNOISSEUR'S PALATE FOR THE SUBTLETIES OF FISH AND MOLLUSKS.

A SPECIAL BODY OF WATER IN SENEGAL IS THE "LAC ROSE" OR PINK LAKE ("RETBA" IN WOLOF), LOCATED IN THE GARDEN BELT (PP. 84, 85). THE LAKE IS A VIBRANT PINK DUE TO FELDSPAR DEPOSITS THAT REFLECT SUNLIGHT THROUGH THE SALTY WATER. THE REMAINS OF A FOSSIL SEA THAT ONCE OCCUPIED ALL OF SENEGAL, THE PINK LAKE HAS BECOME A MAJOR TOURIST ATTRACTION—SPECTACULAR TO SEE AT DAWN OR DUSK. WOMEN COLLECT SALT FROM THE WATER, WHICH MEN TRANSPORT AND SELL. LOCAL WOLOF VILLAGERS LONG THOUGHT THE LAKE WAS HAUNTED AT NIGHT, BUT NEVER MOVED AWAY, AS THE SALT THEY EXTRACTED WAS, AND STILL IS, A VITAL SOURCE OF INCOME.

AKIHIRO YAMAMURA'S PHOTOGRAPHS NOT ONLY GIVE A VIEW OF SENEGAL'S SEDUCTIVE LANDSCAPE, THEY CONVEY THE UNIQUE POWER AND GRACE OF THE SENEGALESE PEOPLE. THE BUOYANT, CREATIVE SPIRIT OF MY WEST AFRICAN COUNTRY IS WELL-KNOWN; YAMAMURA'S PICTURES CONVEY THAT SPIRIT, AND ALSO THIS: THAT SENEGAL IS A CULTURE EMBRACING MODERN LIFE WITHOUT FORSAKING ITS PAST, A HUMANE, MAJESTIC COMMUNITY ROOTED IN MUTUAL RESPECT AND HARMONY.

DR. MOHAMED MBODJ

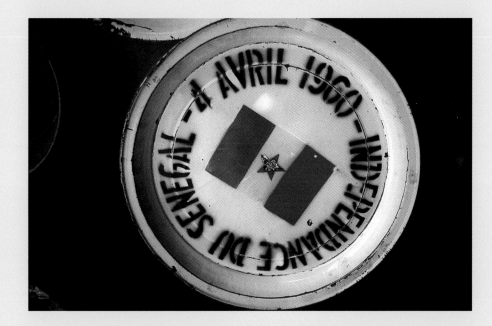

Matam, 1993

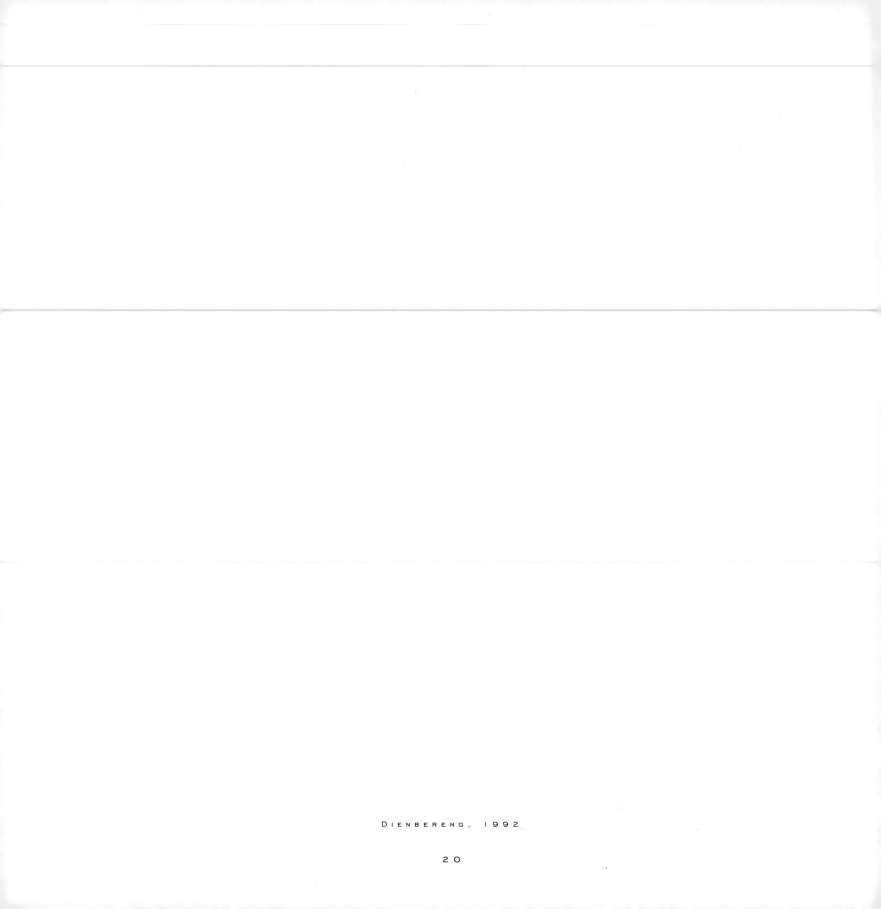

DIENBERENG, 1992

Matam, 1993

23

JOAL-FADIONT, 1989

26

JOAL-FADIONT, 1989

27

M L O M P ,   1 9 9 2

MATAM, 1993

30

MAKO, 1992

31

ZIGUINCHOR, 1989

33

MLOMP, 1992

PHOTOGRAPHS ON PAGES 38 AND 39
THIES 1993

PHOTOGRAPHS ON PAGES 40 AND 41
JOAL-FABIOUT, 1989

FIMELA, 1993

CAP-SKIRING, 1992

KAOLAK, 1992

43

MDOUR, 1989

CARABANE, 1989

45

MLOMP, 1992

Mako, 1992

47

Matam, 1993

49

ELINKINDE, 1989

JOAL-FADIONT, 1992

51

DAKAR, 1992

DAKAR, 1992

54

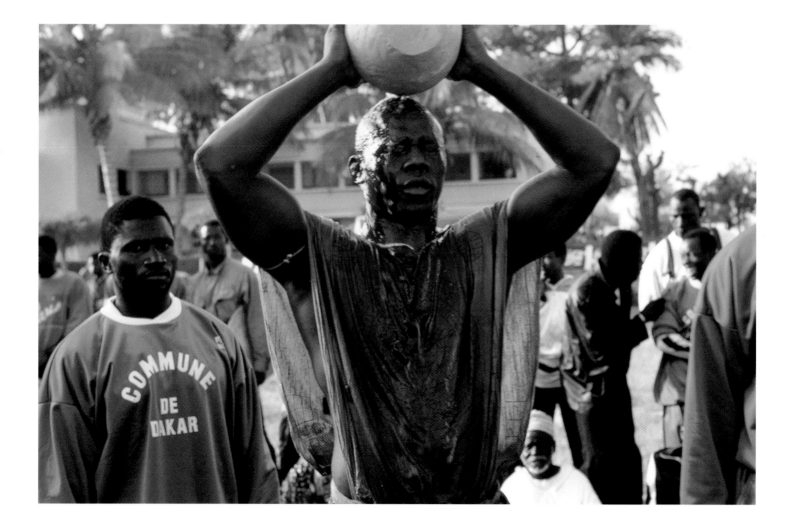

DAKAR, 1992

55

JOAL-FADIOUT, 1993

57

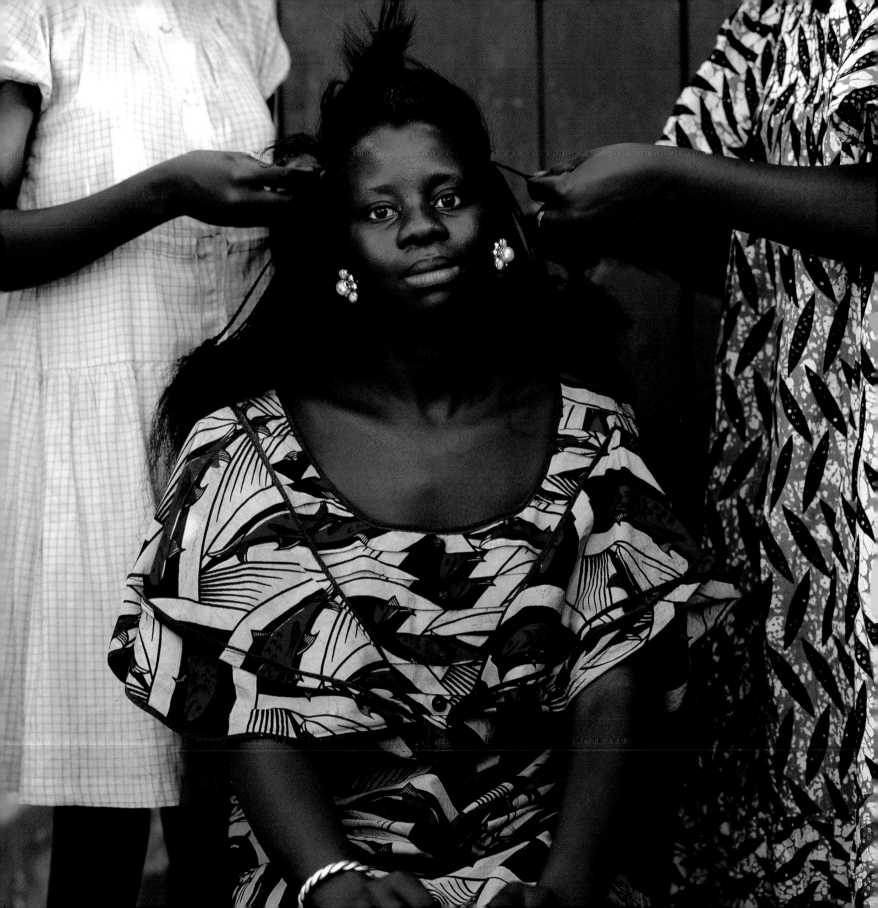

JOAL-FADIOUT, 1992

61

PHOTGRAPHS ON PAGE 64 FROM LEFT TO RIGHT

FIRST ROW

OUSSOUYE, 1992

JOAL-FADIOUT, 1992

BOUKOT OUTLOF, 1992

BOUKOT OUTLOF, 1992

SECOND ROW

BOUKOT OUTLOF, 1992

BOUKOT OUTLOF, 1992

JOAL-FADIOUT, 1992

BOUKOT OUTLOF, 1992

THIRD ROW

KIDIRA, 1993

MLOMP, 1992

BOUKOT OUTLOF, 1992

BOUKOT OUTLOF, 1992

PHOTOGRAPHS ON PAGE 65 FROM LEFT TO RIGHT

FIRST ROW

BOUKOT OUTLOF, 1992

JOAL-FADIOUT, 1989

BOUKOT OUTLOF, 1992

BOUKOT OUTLOF, 1992

SECOND ROW

DAKAR, 1992

BOUKOT OUTLOF, 1992

MLOMP, 1992

BOUKOT OUTLOF, 1992

THIRD ROW

BOUKOT OUTLOF, 1992

BOUKOT OUTLOF, 1992

BOUKOT OUTLOF, 1992

BOUKOT OUTLOF, 1992

DAKAR, 1993

63

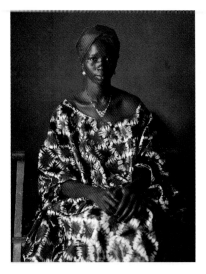   

DAKAR, 1989

66

Dakar, 1992

PINK LAKE [DAKAR], 1993

DAKAR, 1993

ELINKIND, 1989

75

THIES, 1993

77

PHOTGRAPHS ON PAGE 82

MBOUR, 1989

PHOTOGRAPH ON PAGE 83

SEDHIOW, 1993

Dakar, 1989

PINK LAKE [DAKAR], 1993

PINK LAKE [DAKAR], 1993

Thies, 1993

87

GORÉE ISLAND, 1993

CARABANE, 1989

91

Photograph on pages 94 and 95
Dakar, 1993

Photographs on pages 96 and 97
Dakar, 1993

Photograph on facing page
Joal- Fadiout, 1992

92

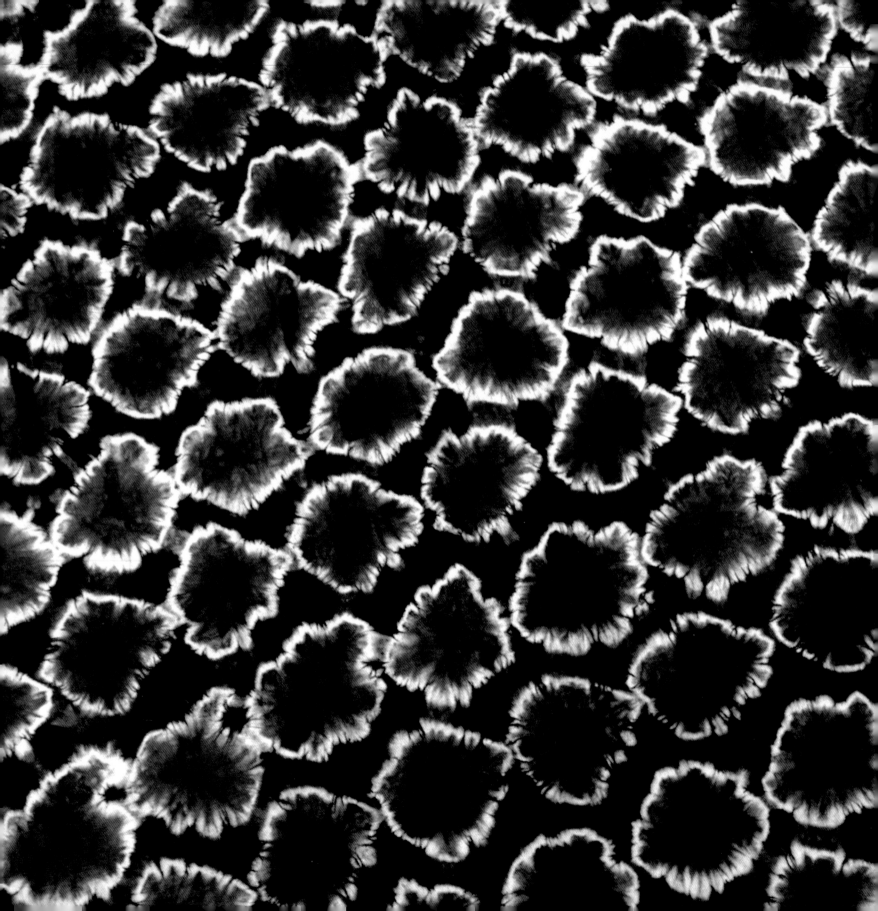

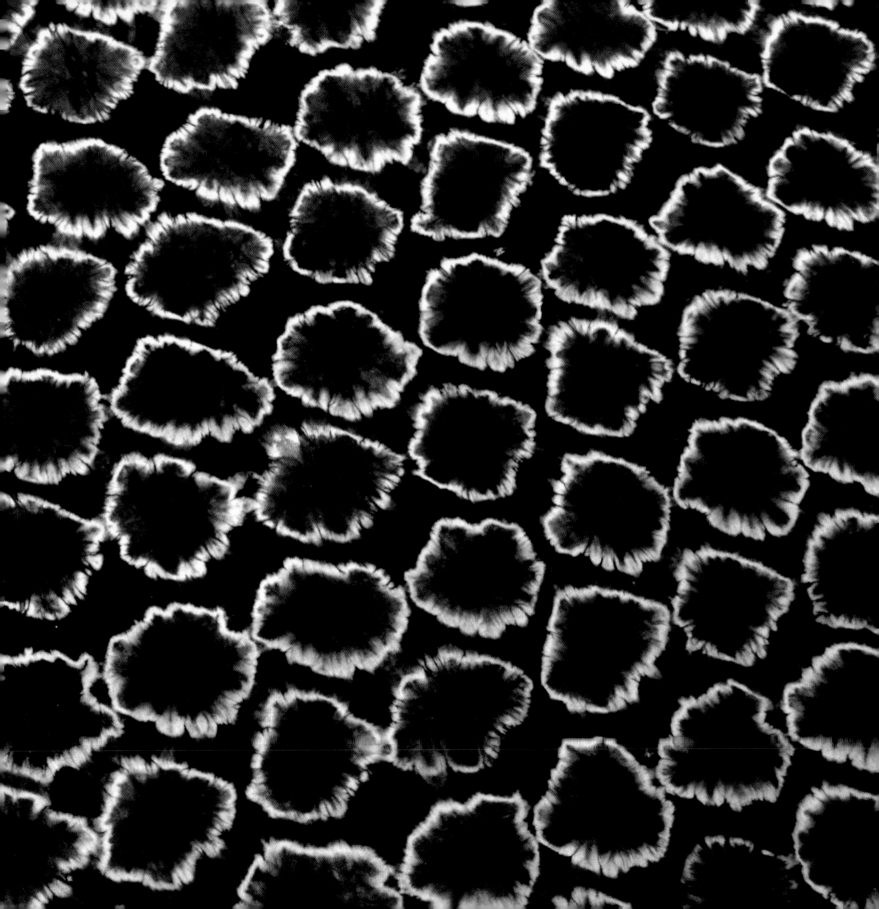

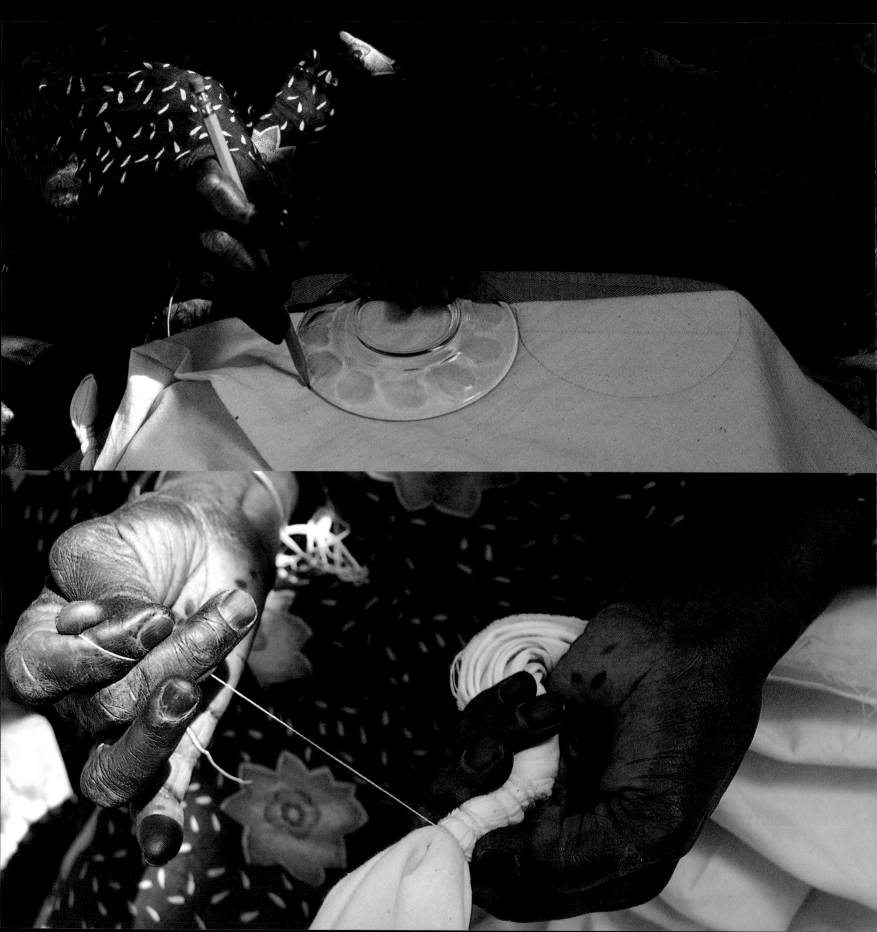

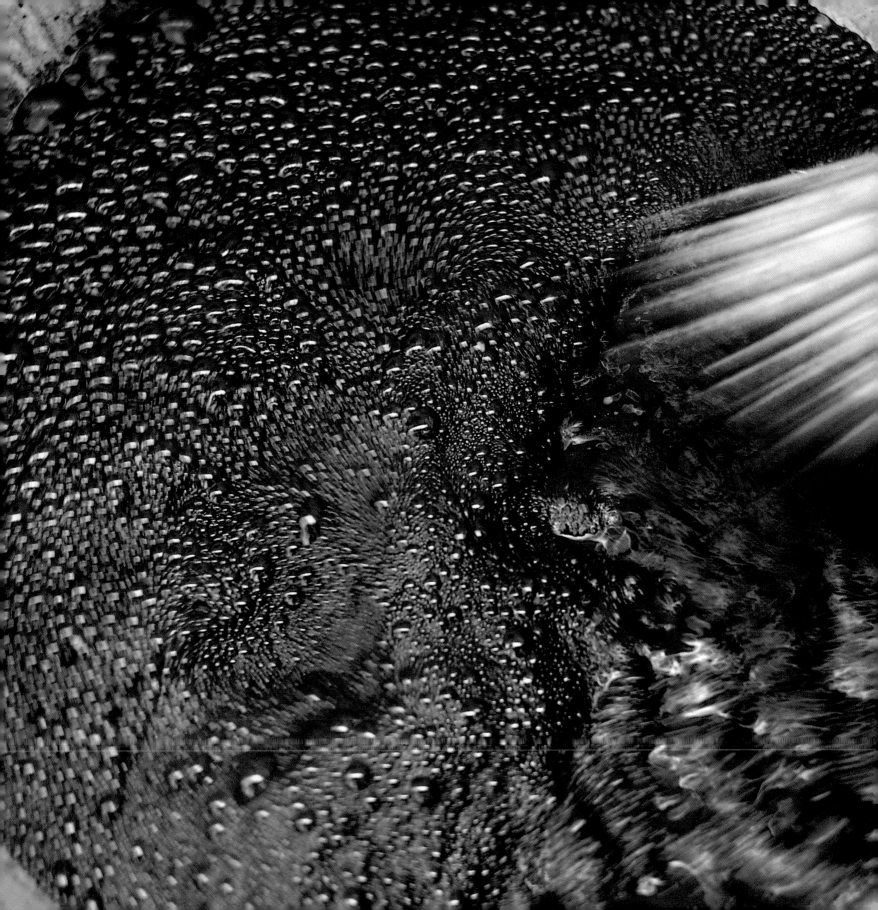

DAKAR. 1993

KABROUSE, 1993

KEDOUGOU, 1992

103

MLOMP, 1989

BRIN, 1992

105

Gorée Island, 1989

Elinkinde, 1989

111